Meet Jasmin

Little Sister,
forever

AMY OLSON

Balboa Press books may be ordered through booksellers or by contacting:

Balboa Press
A Division of Hay House
1663 Liberty Drive
Bloomington, IN 47403
www.balboapress.com
1 (877) 407-4847

Illustrated by Jess Regan

ISBN: 978-1-9822-3255-9 (sc)
ISBN: 978-1-9822-3256-6 (e)

Library of Congress Control Number: 2019911236

Print information available on the last page.

Balboa Press rev. date: 08/15/2019

BALBOA
PRESS
A DIVISION OF HAY HOUSE

Meet Jasmin

Little Sister, forever

AMY OLSON

Dedicated to my best girls,
Savannah and Jasmin,
and to siblings everywhere.

Acknowledgments and gratitude to my husband, Lance, our parents and family, April Smidl, Cal's Angels, David Barhydt & Judith Matz, Dr. Ellen Albertson, Jennifer Young, and Megan Gertz for their encouragement and priceless advice.

I am four years old. I am a little sister.

My name is Jasmin. It means "gift from God."

I love my name. It is special to me because my big sister picked it out. My mom says my big sister watched a lot of Disney's *Aladdin* the week before I was born.

My big sister is also special to me. She is my only sister, and I do not have any brothers.

My big sister would be seven years old. She is gone though. She died from cancer. Cancer is a sickness in your body.

My big sister was three when she first became sick. I was only a baby.

My big sister had medicine called chemotherapy for her cancer.

Chemotherapy and *cancer* are big words, aren't they? I know them because I hear them all the time.

When my big sister came home from the hospital after her first chemotherapy session, her hair was gone. Did that happen to your sibling, too?

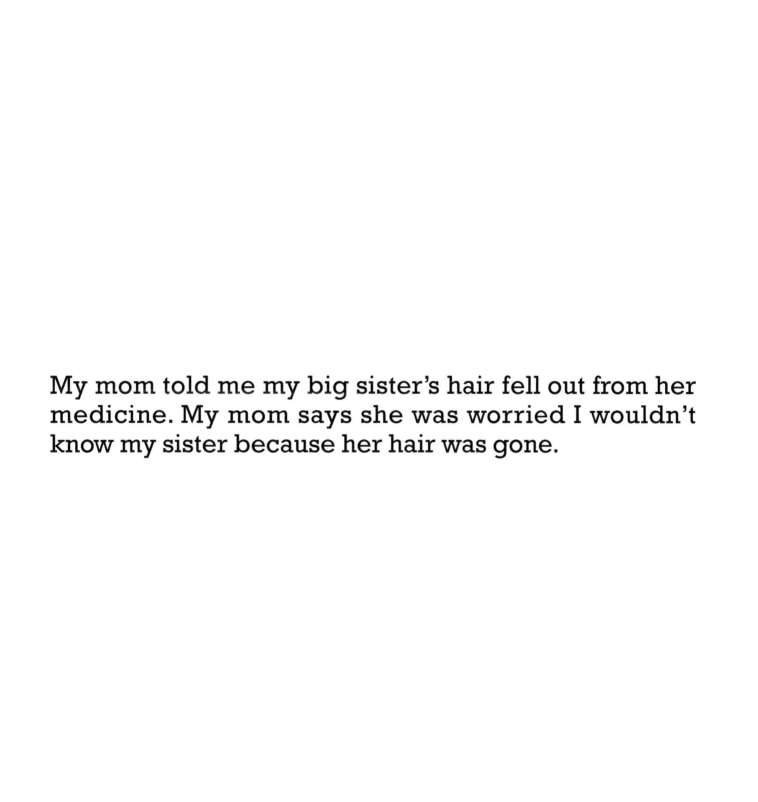

My mom told me my big sister's hair fell out from her medicine. My mom says she was worried I wouldn't know my sister because her hair was gone.

But when my big sister walked in the door, I toddled over to her while my dad held her out to me and said, "Here she is!"

I smiled my best smile. I knew my big sister right away. I was happy she was home.

After that, my big sister was in the hospital a lot for chemotherapy and the cancer.

Were your siblings in the hospital a lot, too?

My mom stayed at the hospital with my big sister. I missed them when they were there.

I bet you missed your brother or sister, too.

My dad would go to the hospital after work to see my big sister and my mom. My dad would come home at night to be with me, but I wanted us all to be together.

Sometimes my dad would bring me to the hospital to play with my big sister and to see my mom. I loved going to see my big sister.

Did you visit your brother or sister in the hospital, too?

When I went to the hospital my big sister would have gifts for me. She liked to do arts and crafts at the hospital. She would draw and paint pictures for me.

I would bring her drawings and paintings home with me to decorate my bedroom.

My big sister also would let me climb into her hospital bed with her.

We would raise the bed up and down. We would color and play doctor together. I would make funny faces and be silly to make her laugh.

My big sister liked to ride around the hospital on her IV stand. My mom would push her. My big sister let me ride along, too. I liked doing what she did because I could be with her.

The doctors and nurses all knew my name. They would be happy I was there to visit my big sister and my mom. They would hug me and give me stickers and other little treats, just like they would give my big sister.

Did you meet your brother or sister's doctors and nurses, too?

When my big sister became tired, my dad and I would go home. I always wanted to stay. My dad would cheer me up in the car on the way home by playing my favorite songs.

But I was most happy when my big sister was home from the hospital.

I liked it when my big sister, my mom, my dad, and I sat on the couch all together.

We were a family then.

We also were a family at the dinner table. I would make my funny faces to see my big sister and my parents laugh.

My mom would say that not only did my name mean "gift from God," but that I also was a gift because I brought joy to our family. She still tells me that today.

Do you know you are a gift, too?

We had fun when our parents would take us on trips if the doctors said my big sister could go. My parents said we needed some fun and time together.

When my big sister was at home, she would play with me when she was not tired or feeling sick.

One game we liked to play was airplane. We would load up our sofa with dolls, dolls' clothes, blankets, and stuffed animals and pretend we were on an airplane going on vacation.

What did your brother or sister play with you?

My big sister would teach me things. Before she died, she taught me how to write my name.

What did your brother or sister teach you?

I miss my big sister. I try not to be sad.

My mom says I should cry when I feel like it and not bottle it up.

But my parents are sad, and I do not want them to worry for me.

I like to do things to help me feel less sad. Taking a nap in my big sister's bed or wearing her clothes helps me feel less sad and lonely.

My parents also let me play with big sister's toys and dolls. I take care of them for her.

Whenever I write my name I feel better because I remember my big sister named me and taught me how to write my name.

My name is Jasmin.

I am four years old.

I am a little sister.

About the Author

AMY OLSON resides in Downers Grove, Illinois with her husband, Lance. The story of this book started in December 2000 when Amy and Lance were enjoying creating memories and traditions for their young family. Savannah, their eldest daughter, was three years old and loved helping take care of her baby sister, Jasmin, when she was diagnosed with diffuse anaplastic Wilm's Tumor, Stage 2. Savannah was in and out of treatment over the next three years. In March 2004, after her fourth relapse, Savannah passed away at age six. Having been by Savannah's side throughout, Jasmin began the long journey of coping without her sister. Amy and Lance modeled their lives after Lance's own bereaved parents by showing Jasmin that family ties, love and life continue. Life did go on. Amy even attended law school and became an attorney after Savannah died. Yet, bereavement is a fickle character. At age 19, Jasmin's journey as a little sister who misses her big sister continues. Amy wrote this children's book with the hope that other siblings who have suffered loss will feel a connection with Jasmin and know they are not alone.

About the Illustrator

JESS REGAN lives in Manteno, Illinois with her family and two dogs. She is a childhood cancer survivor herself and was excited to be able to contribute to such a meaningful project. She has loved drawing since she was little and used her love of drawing to cope with her illness. This book was an incredible opportunity to use that passion to help kids and families just like her own. In her free time, Jess enjoys shopping, watching TV, and spending time with her family and friends. She currently attends Columbia College Chicago and studies Design.

Printed in the United States
By Bookmasters